IMAGINATION is EVERYTHING

This Book Belongs To:

_____

This is a work of fiction. Names, characters, places, and incidents either are the product of the author's imagination or are used fictitiously. Any resemblance to actual persons, living or dead, events, or locales is entirely coincidental.

Copyright © 2022 by Katie Gigliotti

All rights reserved. No part of this book may be reproduced or used in any manner without written permission of the copyright owner except for the use of quotations in a book review. For more information, address: katie@katiegigliotti.com.

First paperback edition March, 2022

Book written, illustrated, and designed by Katie Gigliotti

LCCN: 2022901938

ISBN 978-1-7374300-1-8 paperback
ISBN 978-1-7374300-0-1 hardback

For more information or free printables, visit:
www.katiegigliotti.com

FOR GRANDPA
STANLEY BADOWSKI;
A TRUE CHILD AT HEART.

FOR GWEN & ZANDER

WANDER WORLD

Katie Gigliotti

When visiting Grandma and Grandpa one day, there was nothing to do and I wanted to play.

But playing is never much fun on your own. In a house full of people, I felt all alone.

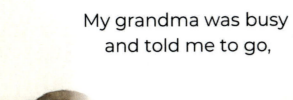

My grandma was busy and told me to go,

and my auntie was watching her favorite show.

Then, from the room over, I heard a loud snore.
So, I peeked through the keyhole and opened the door.

My grandpa lie sleeping in his comfy chair.
I ran over, woke him, and ruffled his hair.

"Let's go on a trip now,"
I said with a smile.
"'Cuz we haven't gone
anywhere for quite a while."

Then, grabbing his hand I pulled up and toward
the big comfy couch where we both climbed aboard.

We strapped on our seat belts excited to play.
Now, we're ready for takeoff. Up, up, and away!

Then, Grandpa asked
brightly, "just where
shall we go?"
and I said "don't be silly...

We'll build a big fort and pack snowballs tight,
and when I shout ready start our epic fight!

Then when I win,
which I certainly will,
we'll both grab our sleds

Far down the hill by an igloo we'll sit,
we will light up a fire to warm up a bit.

We'll gaze at the ocean, at mountains of white,
and a sky full of colors that light up the night.

"Oh, can we go home now?" my grandpa will wonder,

No, no, not quite yet...

We'll swim through the wondrous Great Barrier Reef where we might meet a shark who has one hundred teeth!

Of course he'll be friendly and give us a ride on his slippery back holding tight as we glide.

We'll meet all his friends as we dive down so deep, and then gather some beautiful seashells to keep.

Then, back on the shore with a pail and a rake, an enormous sandcastle we'll happily make.

We'll build it with water and sand til it's done, and then lie on our beach towels and soak up the sun.

And now that they love me, the mermaids and fish will crown me their princess and grant me one wish.

"What's your wish?" Grandpa asked and I said "I'm not sure."

Perhaps, I will wish for...

an AFRICAN tour!

AFRICA

Out there, we'll see lions
with big fluffy manes
who will chase around
zebras on wide open plains.

Then, with our field glasses
we'll watch them all run, as
they frolic about in the African sun.

And when they grow thirsty, they'll all take a stroll
where they gather and drink 'round the watering hole.

While we both lie down in tall, billowy grass
and discover the shapes in the clouds as they pass.

it's **VENICE, ITALY!**

EUROPE

Past houses on water, down canals we'll ride,

while the gondolier paddles and sings loud with pride.

We'll soon disembark and begin down the street
as we say a hello to the people we meet.
At a charming cafe we will stop and relax,
where we'll sip on some coffee and nibble on snacks.

We'll tour through
the buildings
from so long ago,
while you try to teach
me all that you know.

"Is it time to go?" Grandpa asks.
Sure, we will.

But first we must take...

a quick trip to BRAZIL!

Just think of the wonders that we can uncover.
So many new species that we will discover.
Looking glass out, we'll explore every nook for some different life forms to record in our book.

High up above the thick canopy sways as it shelters us both from the sun's burning rays.
Later that day, after trekking so long, from all kinds of birds, we will hear a sweet song.

The song that they sing is my favorite, of course,

we'll join along too
and be part of the chorus.
Then, when our voices
will no longer work,

we'll flee from the jungle....

The buildings all look like they're touching sky, as ten thousand people rush busily by.

We'll hop on a ferry to see all the sights like the Statue of Liberty from water at night.

"So, can we go home yet?"
Grandpa sighs. Oh, no, no.

Let's continue our journey...

We'll land in Nepal and seek out a tour guide.
Far across barren land, we will take a Jeep ride.

From bottom to top, we will take many steps.
When we get halfway up, we will stop for a rest.

We'll camp with some climbers whose goal is the same, and there we'll trade stories and play a few games.

And after we wake, we'll continue our quest until reaching the summit of Mount Everest.

Up at the top, we will see the great sight of our plane swooping down for our very last flight.

Whew, what an adventure! It's time to be done...

'cuz Grandma is waiting and dinner's begun.

We both sat there eating without much to say until Grandma asked,

"Well, what did you do today?"

About the Author

Like her grandfather before her, Katie Gigliotti is a child at heart who wishes that her stories and pictures will inspire young minds to dream, hope, wish, love, and wonder. She has worked as an art educator for more years than she'd like to admit and one day hopes to actually wander the world. When she's not writing, illustrating, or teaching, she enjoys warm summer days, eating junk food, and daydreaming. She lives in a small Virginia town with her husband and two teenage children, whom this book is dedicated to.

Learn more at: katiegigliotti.com

Made in the USA
Columbia, SC
02 April 2022